DANGEROUS
...OR NOT?

SPIDERS

AND OTHER
ARTHROPODS

TRACIE SANTOS

Rourke
Educational Media

A Division of

Carson
Dellosa
Education®

Before Reading: *Building Background Knowledge and Vocabulary*

Building background knowledge can help children process new information and build upon what they already know. Before reading a book, it is important to tap into what children already know about the topic. This will help them develop their vocabulary and increase their reading comprehension.

Questions and Activities to Build Background Knowledge:

1. Look at the front cover of the book and read the title. What do you think this book will be about?
2. What do you already know about this topic?
3. Take a book walk and skim the pages. Look at the table of contents, photographs, captions, and bold words. Did these text features give you any information or predictions about what you will read in this book?

Vocabulary: *Vocabulary Is Key to Reading Comprehension*

Use the following directions to prompt a conversation about each word.

- Read the vocabulary words.
- What comes to mind when you see each word?
- What do you think each word means?

Vocabulary Words:
- *allergic*
- *arthropods*
- *parasite*
- *prey*
- *transmit*
- *venom*

During Reading: *Reading for Meaning and Understanding*

To achieve deep comprehension of a book, children are encouraged to use close reading strategies. During reading, it is important to have children stop and make connections. These connections result in deeper analysis and understanding of a book.

Close Reading a Text

During reading, have children stop and talk about the following:

- Any confusing parts
- Any unknown words
- Text to text, text to self, text to world connections
- The main idea in each chapter or heading

Encourage children to use context clues to determine the meaning of any unknown words. These strategies will help children learn to analyze the text more thoroughly as they read.

When you are finished reading this book, turn to the next-to-last page for **After Reading Questions** and an **Activity**.

TABLE OF CONTENTS

WHAT MAKES AN ARTHROPOD DANGEROUS?

What do you think of when you think of dangerous **arthropods**? You might think of stabbing fangs or dangerous claws. The facts may surprise you.

 arthropods (AHR-thruh-pahdz): animals without backbones that have hard outer skeletons and three or more pairs of legs that can bend

4

Some arthropods can be dangerous to other animals or the environment. Others can cause a lot of destruction.

SHARP FANGS AND GIANT STINGERS

Funnel web spiders have large fangs. Their **venom** can kill an adult person in 24 hours. They sometimes fall into swimming pools and bite when they are taken out.

A Cure for Bites

A cure for funnel web spider venom was made in 1981. No humans have died from a funnel web spider bite since then.

 venom (VEN-uhm): poison put into a victim's body with a bite or sting

LOW HIGH

DANGER METER

Asian giant hornets are the largest hornets in the world. Their venom is dangerous enough to kill someone. They are most dangerous if the person is **allergic**.

 allergic (uh-LUR-jik): the tendency to have an unpleasant reaction, such as getting a rash or having trouble breathing

Quite a Sting

An Asian giant hornet's stinger is about a quarter of an inch (6 millimeters) long!

LOW   HIGH
DANGER METER

11

Tsetse flies eat by sucking blood from animals or humans. The flies can **transmit** diseases. These diseases can be deadly to humans, cows, and other living things.

Sleeping Sickness

One disease transmitted by tsetse flies is sleeping sickness. It is caused by a **parasite**. It sometimes makes people sleep during the day and stay up at night.

 transmit (trans-MIT): to send from one place to another

LOW   HIGH
DANGER METER

 parasite (PAR-uh-site): an animal or plant that lives on or inside of another animal or plant

13

14

Termites chew on wood and other building materials. They can cause billions of dollars in damage each year in the United States. They can damage living trees and shrubs. But they do not bite humans or animals.

LOW   HIGH
DANGER METER

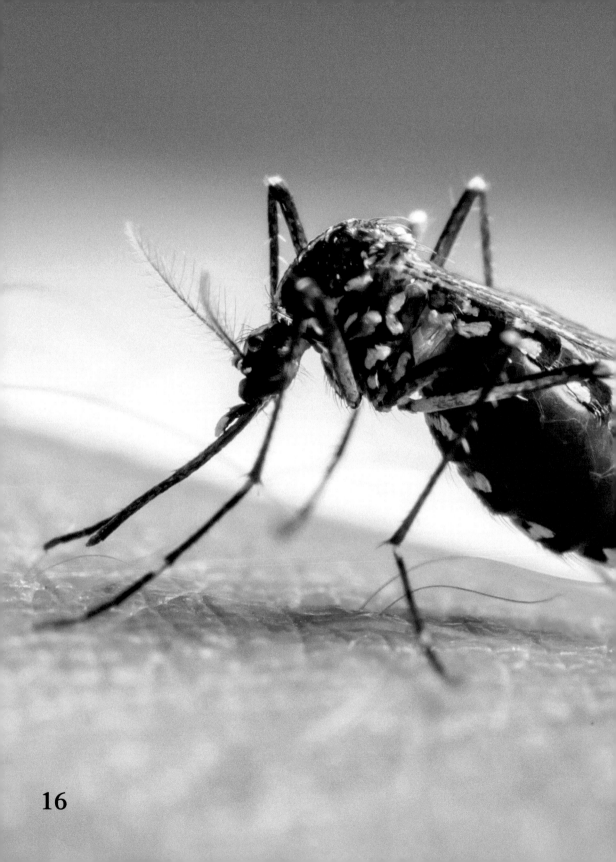

Mosquitoes bite animals and people and suck their blood. They transmit deadly diseases to other living things. Mosquitoes have killed up to 50 billion people throughout history.

LOW   HIGH
DANGER METER

Giant centipedes can be as big as a person's arm. They hunt **prey** on land. Some can even swim! Their venom will not hurt a person, but their bites can cause pain.

 prey (pray): an animal hunted by another animal for food

LOW **HIGH**

DANGER METER

ALL HISS, NO BITE

Madagascar hissing cockroaches might look scary. They are large and hiss when threatened. However, they eat mostly plants and do not attack.

LOW   HIGH

DANGER METER

A Pet WHAT?

Some people keep
Madagascar hissing
cockroaches as pets.
Cockroaches are
easy to take care of.

Animals called harvestmen or cellar spiders are actually two kinds of animals. One is not a spider at all! It is a different kind of animal that looks like a spider. It does not have any venom.

LOW   HIGH
DANGER METER

The other kind of harvestman is a true spider. It hardly ever bites. It has very mild venom.

LOW HIGH
DANGER METER

25

LOW   HIGH

DANGER METER

Stag beetles look scary with their large jaws. The males wrestle each other during mating season. However, stag beetles do not attack otherwise.

Insect Artist

Spike the stag beetle could draw pictures with markers.
He made many drawings by himself and became famous!

Think about the arthropods around you. How are they like the animals in this book? How are they different? What do you think: Are they dangerous...or not?

? LOW HIGH
DANGER METER

? LOW HIGH
DANGER METER

MEMORY GAME

at the pictures. What do you remembe
ng on the pages where each image app

INDEX

AFTER READING QUESTIONS

1. Why are mosquitoes so dangerous?
2. How could an arthropod be dangerous without attacking humans?
3. Why are some spider bites less dangerous than others?
4. What are harvestmen?
5. What makes Asian giant hornets especially dangerous to some people?

ACTIVITY

Pick one of the arthropods in this book. Imagine that you find it in the wild. How dangerous is the arthropod? Describe how you would stay safe around it.

ABOUT THE AUTHOR

Tracie Santos loves learning and writing about animals. She has worked in zoos and aquariums with some of the world's most dangerous animals. She lives in Columbus, Ohio, with her two hairless cats, who are not dangerous but look very strange.

www.rourkeeducationalmedia.com

PHOTO CREDITS: Cover, page 1: ©Kathy Keifer; pages 4-5: ©Ken Griffiths; pages 6-7: ©chaiyon021; pages 8-9, 30: ©Sharath V Jois; pages 10-11, 30: ©Ruzy Hartini; pages 12-13: ©Attardog; pages 14-15: ©TommyIX; pages 16-17, 30: ©smuay; pages 18-19, 30: ©skifbook; pages 20-21: ©torook; pages 22-23, 30: ©frank600; pages 24-25: ©tsvibrav; pages 26-27, 30: ©Mark Brandon; page 28a: ©Linas Toleikis; page 28b: ©Risto0; page 29a: ©comzeal; page 29b: ©SL_Photography; page 32: ©Taryn Lindsey

Edited by: Kim Thompson
Cover design by: Rhea Magaro-Wallace
Interior design by: Bobbie Houser

Library of Congress PCN Data

Spiders and Other Arthropods / Tracie Santos
  (Dangerous...or Not?)
  ISBN 978-1-73163-822-9 (hard cover)
  ISBN 978-1-73163-899-1 (soft cover)
  ISBN 978-1-73163-976-9 (e-Book)
  ISBN 978-1-73164-053-6 (e-Pub)
Library of Congress Control Number: 2020930195

Rourke Educational Media
Printed in the United States of America
02-1062411937